D0745466

APR   2013

AFRICAN-AMERICAN ACTIVISTS

CAROL ELLIS

TITLES IN THIS SERIES

AFRICAN-AMERICAN ACTIVISTS

CAROL ELLIS

MASON CREST
PHILADELPHIA

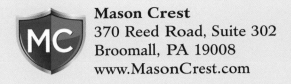

Mason Crest
370 Reed Road, Suite 302
Broomall, PA 19008
www.MasonCrest.com

Printed and bound in the United States of America.

CPSIA Compliance Information: Batch #MBC2012-1. For further information, contact Mason Crest at 1-866-MCP-Book.

First printing
1 3 5 7 9 8 6 4 2

Library of Congress Cataloging-in-Publication Data

Ellis, Carol, 1945-
  African American activists / Carol Ellis.
      p. cm. — (Major Black contributions from emancipation to civil rights)
  Includes bibliographical references.
  ISBN 978-1-4222-2371-0 (hardcover)
  ISBN 978-1-4222-2384-0 (pbk.)
  1. African Americans—Civil rights—History—Juvenile literature. 2. African Americans—Politics and government—Juvenile literature. 3. Civil rights movements—United States—History—Juvenile literature. 4. African American civil rights workers—Biography—Juvenile literature. 5. African American political activists—Biography—Juvenile literature. 6. United States—Race relations—History—Juvenile literature. I. Title.
  E185.E395 2012
  323.1196'073—dc23
                                                      2011051944

Publisher's note: All quotations in this book are taken from original sources, and contain the spelling and grammatical inconsistencies of the original texts.

Picture credits: The George F. Landegger Collection of District of Columbia Photographs in Carol M. Highsmith's America, Library of Congress, Prints and Photographs Division: 13; Booker T. Washington Papers, Manuscript Division, Library of Congress: 18; Library of Congress: 8, 10, 14, 15, 16, 17, 21, 23, 24, 26, 28, 30, 32, 36, 37, 40, 42, 43, 45, 46, 47, 49; LBJ Library photo by Yoichi Okamoto: 48; courtesy Robert Russa Moton Museum: 35; Ryan Rodrick Beiler / Shutterstock.com: 54; Ira Bostic / Shutterstock.com: 3, 53; Featureflash / Shutterstock.com: 50; Steve Heap / Shutterstock.com: 7.

TABLE OF CONTENTS

INTRODUCTION

Dr. Marc Lamont Hill

It is impossible to tell the story of America without telling the story of Black Americans. From the struggle to end slavery, all the way to the election of the first Black president, the Black experience has been a window into America's own movement toward becoming a "more perfect union." Through the tragedies and triumphs of Blacks in America, we gain a more full understanding of our collective history and a richer appreciation of our collective journey. This book series, MAJOR BLACK CONTRIBUTIONS FROM EMANCIPATION TO CIVIL RIGHTS, spotlights that journey by showing the many ways that Black Americans have been a central part of our nation's development.

In this series, we are reminded that Blacks were not merely objects of history, swept up in the winds of social and political inevitability. Rather, since the end of legal slavery, Black men and women have actively fought for their own rights and freedoms. It is through their courageous efforts (along with the efforts of allies of all races) that Blacks are able to enjoy ever increasing levels of inclusion in American democracy. Through this series, we learn the names and stories of some of the most important contributors to our democracy.

But this series goes far beyond the story of slavery to freedom. The books in this series also demonstrate the various contributions of Black Americans to the nation's social, cultural, technological, and intellectual growth. While these books provide new and deeper insights into the lives and stories of familiar figures like Martin Luther King, Michael Jordan, and Oprah Winfrey, they also introduce readers to the contributions of countless heroes who have often been pushed to the margins of history. In reading this series, we are able to see that Blacks have been key contributors across every field of human endeavor.

Although this is a series about Black Americans, it is important and necessary reading for everyone. While readers of color will find enormous purpose and pride in uncovering the history of their ancestors, these books should also create similar sentiments among readers of all races and ethnicities. By understanding the rich and deep history of Blacks, a group often ignored or marginalized in history, we are reminded that everyone has a story. Everyone has a contribution. Everyone matters.

The insights of these books are necessary for creating deeper, richer, and more inclusive classrooms. More importantly, they remind us of the power and possibility of individuals of all races, places, and traditions. Such insights not only allow us to understand the past, but to create a more beautiful future.

Frederick Douglass (1818–1895) escaped from slavery to become a national figure who spoke and wrote eloquently about the injustice of slavery.

1

BECOMING FREE

It was the night of January 1, 1863. The United States was in the middle of the Civil War. Eleven southern states had seceded from the Union. They had formed a separate government called the Confederacy. The Federal government was fighting to bring the rebellious states back into the Union.

On that January night, hundreds of people crowded into the Tremont Temple in Boston, Massachusetts. Messengers waited between the church and the nearest telegraph office. They wanted to deliver the news as fast as they could.

"We were waiting and listening as for a bolt from the sky," wrote an African American named Frederick Douglass. "Eight, nine, ten o'clock came and went, and still no word."

Six months earlier, President Abraham Lincoln had given the Confederate states a warning: surrender to the Union by January 1, or your slaves will be set free. But the Confederate states didn't give up. The bloody fighting didn't stop. Now New Year's Day had arrived. Would Lincoln free the slaves?

Douglass waited anxiously with the rest of the people in the church. "At last . . . a man with hasty step advanced through the crowd," he wrote, "and . . . exclaimed in tones that thrilled all hearts, 'It is coming!' 'It is on the wires!!'"

The telegraph wires carried good news: President Lincoln had issued the Emancipation Proclamation. It declared that "all persons held as slaves within [states in rebellion] are, and henceforward shall be free."

The people inside the church cheered and cried with joy. They were keen opponents of slavery, or abolitionists. In spite of their joy, the Emancipation Proclamation didn't actually free slaves—at least not yet. The rebellious states refused to free their slaves. Only a Union military victory would force them to do so. Also, there were four slave states—Delaware, Kentucky, Maryland, and Missouri—that hadn't seceded. Because Lincoln didn't want to drive them to the Confederate side, the Emancipation Proclamation didn't apply to slaves in those states. For many abolitionists, this was a huge disappointment. But not for Frederick Douglass. He was sure that the proclamation was a first step to "the entire abolition of slavery." He had been working for an end to slavery for many years. He would keep working, no matter how long it took.

FROM SLAVE TO ACTIVIST

Frederick Douglass was born in Maryland in 1818. He spent the first 20 years of his life as a slave. He was the property of white masters. He worked when and where they told him to. When he was very young, he was sent to Baltimore to work for a ship's carpenter. His master's wife began to teach him to read. Her husband was furious. It was against the law for slaves to learn to read and write. If they could read, they might learn that a lot of people were against slavery. If they could write, they could forge papers and escape. The master's wife stopped teaching Douglass, but he didn't stop learning. He asked his white playmates for help. By the time Douglass was 13, he could read and write. Then he began to teach other slaves, even though they all risked getting whipped.

In 1838, Douglass disguised himself in a sailor's uniform and boarded a train. Black sailors had special papers that allowed them to travel. Douglass had gotten his papers and a uniform from a retired sailor. The

This ornate reproduction of the Emancipation Proclamation includes a picture of President Abraham Lincoln. The order, which went into effect on January 1, 1863, declared that slaves living in ten southern states that were in rebellion against the U.S. government were free.

two men didn't look anything like each other. But the train conductor did not bother to read the description carefully. Douglass had escaped! He made his way to the state of Massachusetts. Many people there thought slavery was wrong. They worked for it to be abolished. Frederick Douglass joined them. "I dropped into the ranks of freedom's friends," he wrote, "and went forth to the battle."

SPEAKING OUT

Douglass didn't fight slavery with rifles or cannons. He used words. He began to speak at antislavery meetings in many Northern cities. People said that Frederick Douglass was an amazing speaker. He could be funny as well as serious. He described his life as a slave. He talked of working in the fields from dawn until 11:00 at night. He told how his family was torn apart when they were sent to different plantations. He described being beaten with sticks and whips. Then he reminded people that there were 4 million slaves in the country. And he called for slavery to be completely abolished.

Frederick Douglass was becoming famous. This put him in danger. He had escaped slavery, but he was not legally free. His master in Maryland had the right to send slave hunters to bring him back. Douglass left the United States to speak in England and Ireland. Friends there raised money for him. When he returned to the United States, he was able to buy his freedom.

After a few years, Douglass moved to the city of Rochester, New York. He started a newspaper called the *North Star*. He wrote that slavery was immoral. He said it shouldn't be allowed. When the Civil War started, Douglass said that the Union needed black soldiers to help

= Did You Know? =

Frederick Douglass's house in Rochester, New York, became an important "station," on the Underground Railroad. This was a network of safe houses where runaway slaves could hide as they escaped to the North or Canada. Douglass hid many fugitive slaves in his house.

win the war. He recruited many freed slaves to fight on the Union side. And he argued that they should get the same treatment and the same pay as white soldiers.

Douglass and President Lincoln began to write letters to each other. Lincoln invited Douglass to the White House to talk. The two men first

Frederick Douglass (right) asks President Lincoln and members of his cabinet to enlist African Americans into the American army and navy. Ultimately, more than 186,000 African Americans would fight for the Union during the Civil War.

Two of the African-American soldiers who fought in the Civil War.

met in the summer of 1863. Lincoln invited Douglass back to the White House the following year. They didn't completely agree on how the war should be conducted. In the North, many people were growing weary of all the bloodshed. Some questioned whether the cost of ending slavery was too high. Lincoln hated slavery. But he wanted the focus of the war to be on preserving the Union. Douglass thought the fight should be against slavery. However, he became convinced that the president was equally committed to the goal of getting rid of slavery. Douglass believed that slavery would end if the Union won the Civil War.

AFTER THE WAR

In April 1865, the Union did win the war. And, as Frederick Douglass had believed, slavery was soon ended. In December 1865, the states ratified, or approved, the 13th Amendment to the U.S. Constitution. It made slavery illegal everywhere in the United States.

Some abolitionists thought the battle was over. But Douglass knew better. "Slavery is not abolished until the black man has the ballot," he said. Douglass traveled to many Northern cities to speak about voting rights for black men. He warned that former slaveholders were trying to take charge of state governments in

Harriet Tubman (1820?–1913) was nicknamed "Moses" for her furtive work helping African-American slaves escape to the North during the 1850s and 1860s. During the Civil War, Tubman worked as a spy for the Union Army and guided Union troops during an 1863 raid of plantations on the Combahee River in South Carolina that freed some 700 slaves. Later, during the 1890s, Tubman worked with Susan B. Anthony and other Suffragists who sought the right for women to vote.

Reconstruction

The 13th, 14th, and 15th Amendments to the U.S. Constitution are known as the Reconstruction amendments. Reconstruction was a period in U.S. history that lasted from the end of the Civil War in 1865 until 1877. During this time, the defeated Confederate states were reorganized and brought back into the Union.

Among many whites in the South, there was bitter opposition to the idea of giving African Americans equal rights. The Southern states were forced to accept the Reconstruction amendments. But they found ways to prevent blacks from exercising the rights guaranteed by those amendments. For example, the states used a variety of measures to stop black men from voting. One was by making blacks (but not whites) pass a literacy test, to show that they could read and write, before they were allowed to vote. Another was the poll tax, a fee that many African Americans couldn't afford. In many cases, blacks who passed the literacy test and paid the poll tax were still prevented from voting by the threat of violence.

This magazine cover shows newly freed African Americans lining up to vote in an election, 1867.

the South. He warned about hate groups like the Ku Klux Klan. These used intimidation and murder to prevent newly freed blacks from exercising their civil rights.

In 1866, Congress passed the 14th Amendment. It declared that former slaves were full citizens and that no state could deny any citizens their rights. The amendment was ratified in July 1868.

═ *Did You Know?* ═

Frederick Douglass supported voting rights for black men. But he also argued that all women should have the right to vote as well. Women wouldn't be guaranteed the right to vote in the United States until 1920.

The following year, Congress passed the 15th Amendment. It guaranteed all male citizens of every race the right to vote. Ratification occurred in 1870.

"I seem to be living in a new world," a joyful Frederick Douglass declared. Still, Douglass knew his work wasn't done. Black people faced discrimination all over the country. So Frederick Douglass kept writing and speaking for African-American rights until his death in 1895.

Another African-American advocate, Sojourner Truth (1797?–1883), was an abolitionist and supporter of women's rights. She is best known for her 1851 speech "Ain't I a Woman?" delivered at the Ohio Woman's Rights Convention in Akron, Ohio.

ADDRESS BY BOOKER T. WASHINGTON, PRINCIPAL

TUSKEGEE NORMAL AND INDUSTRIAL INSTITUTE, TUSKEGEE, ALABAMA,

AT OPENING OF ATLANTA EXPOSITION,

Sept. 18th, 1895.

Mr. President, Gentlemen of the Board of Directors and Citizens:

One third of the population of the South is of the Negro race. No enterprise seeking the material, civil or moral welfare of this section can disregard this element of our population and reach the highest success. I but convey to you, Mr. President and Directors, the sentiment of the masses of my race, when I say that in no way have the value and manhood of the American Negro been more fittingly and generously recognized, than by the managers of this magnificent Exposition at every stage of its progress. It is a recognition which will do more to cement the friendship of the two races than any occurrence since the dawn of our freedom.

Not only this, but the opportunity here afforded will awaken among us a new era of industrial progress. Ignorant and inexperienced, it is not strange that in the first years of our new life we began at the top instead of the bottom, that a seat in Congress or the State Legislature was more sought t an real-estate or industrial skill, that the political convention, or stump speaking had

The first page of Booker T. Washington's 1895 "Atlanta Compromise" speech, in which the famous activist said that African Americans should not agitate for social and political equality with whites, so long as they received an education and were permitted to work or own businesses. Although this approach was initially supported by both black and white leaders, it did little to improve the condition of African Americans and was eventually criticized by those who wanted blacks to fight more actively for full civil rights, such as W.E.B. Du Bois.

2

COOPERATE OR FIGHT?

By the 1880s, African Americans' prospects for equality were fading fast. The Civil War had done away with slavery. The Constitution had been amended to guarantee civil rights for blacks. In the South, however, whites moved to keep African Americans "in their place." State legislatures passed laws that ensured blacks would remain second-class citizens. White mobs and organized hate groups such as the Ku Klux Klan played an informal role in making sure blacks didn't challenge their unequal status. African Americans living in the South knew they could be seized and murdered at any time for any perceived slight against their white neighbors. Over the years, thousands of blacks were, in fact, lynched.

Conditions for African Americans were worst in the South. But even in the North, blacks faced discrimination.

TWO DIFFERENT APPROACHES

How should black people deal with the injustices they faced? The issue divided the African-American community. On one side were those who were willing to work toward equality little by little. They favored cooperation with white society. On the other side were those who favored a more confrontational approach. They weren't interested in gaining equal rights gradually. They demanded immediate equality. The Constitution, after all, was supposed to guarantee that.

Each approach was championed by a great African-American leader. Booker T. Washington favored the path of cooperation with white society. W. E. B. Du Bois favored direct and forceful opposition to discrimination.

WASHINGTON: THE PATH OF SELF-RELIANCE

Booker T. Washington was born a slave in Franklin County, Virginia, in 1856. He never knew his father. He was raised by his mother in a small log cabin on their master's property.

As a child, Booker worked in the fields and slept on a grain sack. The cabin Booker and his family lived in had no floor and very little furniture. There was almost never enough to eat. There was no time for much of anything but work. This was a normal life for a slave.

When Booker was nine years old, the Civil War ended. Slavery was now illegal. Years later, he recalled the day he and his family heard the news. "My mother, who was by my side, leaned over and kissed her children while tears of joy ran down her cheeks," Washington wrote.

> She explained to us what it all meant, that this was the day for which she had been so long praying, but fearing that she would never live to see.
>
> For some minutes there was great rejoicing, and thanksgiving, and wild scenes of ecstasy. But there was no feeling of bitterness. In fact, there was pity among the slaves for our former owners.

Booker's mother took her children to West Virginia. There she joined her husband. The two had been slaves on different plantations, and it had been some time since they'd seen each other.

Booker's stepfather promptly put him to work at a salt factory to help support the family. The boy soon taught himself numbers and the alphabet. He had a burning desire to learn to read. But when a small school for black children was started nearby, Booker's stepfather wouldn't allow him to attend. He had to work in the salt factory. Booker persisted, though.

Eventually his stepfather agreed to let Booker go to the school if he worked before and after his classes.

For a half dozen years, Booker kept up his studies while working at a series of jobs—in the salt factory, as a coal miner, as a servant in the home of a wealthy white family. When he was 16, he enrolled at the Hampton Institute, a school for African Americans that was founded in 1868. He excelled there.

After graduating from Hampton, Booker T. Washington worked as a teacher. Then, in 1881, he was named head of a new college in Alabama. The school, called the Tuskegee Institute, prepared African Americans to become teachers. But students at Tuskegee also learned skills such as carpentry, brick making, and farming. In fact, the first Tuskegee students used what they learned to build classrooms and grow food for the college. Washington believed these practical skills were very important. They would help blacks become more self-reliant. They would help blacks lift themselves from poverty.

Booker T. Washington (1856–1915) believed it was critical for African Americans to become educated so they could succeed economically in the post–Civil War South.

Washington turned the Tuskegee Institute into one of the top black schools in the country. Many people admired his work there. These included powerful white people, some of whom gave money to Tuskegee. The school grew famous. So did its director.

Washington often spoke out on the issue of race relations. In September 1895, he gave an important speech before a mostly white audience at a trade exposition in Atlanta. In the speech, Washington suggested

how southern whites and blacks could live together in a way that would bring prosperity to both races. Whites, he said, should guarantee that black children had access to basic education. Whites should also give blacks economic opportunities. Blacks, in turn, wouldn't insist on political or social equality. They wouldn't demand civil rights. They wouldn't complain about segregation—the practice of keeping the races separate in public places.

Blacks would simply work hard. Eventually, Washington believed, they would win the trust and goodwill of the white community. That, and the economic and educational gains made by African Americans, would lead to "progress in the enjoyment of all the privileges that will come to us." Among these "privileges" was equality under the law.

For the most part, whites responded enthusiastically to Washington's Atlanta Compromise speech, as it came to be called. Many African Americans, too, were willing to put off political and social equality in favor of educational and economic progress. For a while, Booker T. Washington was the most prominent leader in the African-American community.

DU BOIS: DEMANDING EQUALITY

But the Atlanta Compromise didn't solve the country's racial problems. Southern whites didn't suddenly stop mistreating their black neighbors. African Americans were still attacked and lynched.

Other black leaders felt that Booker T. Washington's path of patient cooperation with whites wasn't working. They wanted to chart an entirely different course. Perhaps the most influential of these black leaders was W. E. B. Du Bois.

William Edward Burghardt Du Bois was born in 1868 in Great Barrington, Massachusetts. He was raised by his mother, who worked as a maid, and by his grandfather. Du Bois attended public school. Almost all his classmates were white, but he didn't experience open racism. He excelled as a student.

After high school, Du Bois went to Fisk University. It was a college for blacks in the southern state of Tennessee. At Fisk, Du Bois first learned about the daily humiliations that many African Americans had to live with. It made him angry. He began writing about the mistreatment of blacks in the school paper.

W.E.B. Du Bois (1868–1963) was a major scholar and activist of the early 20th century.

After graduating from Fisk, Du Bois studied at Harvard University in Massachusetts. Later, he won a scholarship to a university in Germany. There, he learned about the brutal European colonial rule in Africa. It reminded him of the treatment of blacks in the United States.

When he returned from Germany, Du Bois became the first African American awarded a PhD in history from Harvard. He taught at several schools and universities. He wrote about racism and the mistreatment of black Americans.

Du Bois opposed Booker T. Washington's ideas. He argued that African Americans shouldn't wait until white society saw fit to honor their legal rights. Black people shouldn't have to beg for rights other Americans took for granted. Du Bois urged African Americans to be proud of themselves and their culture. He thought that while work was important, education was the key to black empowerment. And he believed that African

The NAACP

The National Association for the Advancement of Colored People (NAACP) is the country's oldest and largest civil rights organization. Formed more than a century ago, it today boasts more than half a million members.

At the time the NAACP was founded, African Americans were being lynched almost weekly. Race riots were on the rise, even in northern cities. In fact, a race riot that rocked the hometown of Abraham Lincoln helped lead to the establishment of the NAACP. That riot broke out in August 1908. It left at least seven people dead and dozens of black homes and businesses destroyed.

In the wake of the Springfield race riot, a group of concerned whites and blacks met in New York City to discuss what might be done to solve the country's racial problems. W. E. B. Du Bois was one of seven African Americans to attend. The February 1909 meeting led to the formation of the NAACP.

The NAACP's goal was to make sure that all people were protected by the 13th, 14th, and 15th Amendments to the Constitution. That remains the core mission of the organization. The NAACP works to end racial discrimination. It promotes equal treatment in education, the workplace, and all areas of society.

Americans who were educated—as he was—had a responsibility to fight for those who were not.

In 1905, Du Bois helped found an organization called the Niagara Movement. Its members were leading black intellectuals, activists, and journalists. They weren't interested in the sort of compromises that Booker T. Washington promoted. They strongly condemned racism. They demanded civil rights for African Americans, and they demanded them right away. "We are men!" Du Bois said. "We want to be treated as men. And we shall win."

The Niagara Movement never had more than about 200 members. And by 1910, it had disbanded. Still, it helped pave the way for a larger and more influential civil rights organization. Du Bois cofounded that organization, the National Association for the Advancement of Colored People (NAACP), in 1909. He launched the NAACP's magazine, *The Crisis*. For many years, he served as editor of the publication. In its pages, Du Bois attacked racism and oppression. He refused to apologize for insisting on racial equality. "I am resolved to be quiet and law abiding," Du Bois wrote in *The Crisis* in 1912, "but to refuse to cringe in body or in soul, to resent deliberate insult, and to assert my just rights in the face of wanton aggression."

W. E. B. Du Bois died in 1963. A year later, President Lyndon Johnson signed the Civil Rights Act. It included many of the reforms Du Bois had championed throughout his long life.

CONSIDER THE FACTS.

During six weeks of the months of March and April just past, twelve colored men were lynched in Georgia, the reign of outlawry culminating in the torture and hanging of the colored preacher, Elijah Strickland, and the burning alive of Samuel Wilkes, alias Hose, Sunday, April 23, 1899.

The real purpose of these savage demonstrations is to teach the Negro that in the South he has no rights that the law will enforce. Samuel Hose was burned to teach the Negroes that no matter what a white man does to them, they must not resist. Hose, a servant, had killed Cranford, his employer. An example must be made. Ordinary punishment was deemed inadequate. This Negro must be burned alive. To make the burning a certainty the charge of outrage was invented, and added to the charge of murder. The daily press offered reward for the capture of Hose and then openly incited the people to burn him as soon as caught. The mob carried out the plan in every savage detail.

Of the twelve men lynched during that reign of unspeakable barbarism, only one was even charged with an assault upon a woman. Yet Southern apologists justify their savagery on the ground that Negroes are lynched only because of their crimes against women.

The Southern press champions burning men alive, and says, "Consider the facts." The colored people join issue and also say, "Consider the facts." The colored people of Chicago employed a detective to go to Georgia, and his report in this pamphlet gives the facts. We give here the details of the lynching as they were reported in the Southern papers, then follows the report of the true facts as to the cause of the lynchings, as learned by the investigation. We submit all to the sober judgment of the Nation, confident that, in this cause, as well as all others, "Truth is mighty and will prevail."

IDA B. WELLS-BARNETT.

2939 Princeton Avenue, Chicago, June 20, 1899.

Lynch Law in Georgia.

BY

IDA B. WELLS-BARNETT

A Six-Weeks' Record in the Center of Southern Civilization, As Faithfully Chronicled by the "Atlanta Journal" and the "Atlanta Constitution."

ALSO THE FULL REPORT OF LOUIS P. LE VIN,

The Chicago Detective Sent to Investigate the Burning of Samuel Hose, the Torture and Hanging of Elijah Strickland, the Colored Preacher, and the Lynching of Nine Men for Alleged Arson.

This Pamphlet is Circulated by Chicago Colored Citizens.
2939 Princeton Avenue, Chicago.

1899

The cover (right) and first page of the 1899 pamphlet *Lynch Law in Georgia*, written by journalist and activist Ida B. Wells-Barnett. Between 1880 and 1900, mob violence in Georgia aimed at African Americans grew steadily. The violence peaked in 1899 when 27 lynchings occurred. Among the most savage was the April 23, 1899, lynching of Sam Hose, a black farmer accused of killing his white employer. A mob removed Hose from jail, tortured him, and burned him at the stake. His charred knuckles were displayed in an Atlanta grocer's store window as a trophy. Ida B. Wells-Barnett and her friends hired Louis P. Le Vin, a white private detective, to investigate Hose's lynching and those of ten other black men.

3

WOMEN WARRIORS

I t wasn't just African-American men who struggled to secure equal rights. Black women, too, took part in that fight. And in one respect, the challenge they faced was even more daunting. They had to overcome unfair treatment based on gender as well as race. The 15th Amendment applied only to men. American women—white and black—wouldn't be guaranteed the right to vote until 1920.

FIGHTING FOR JUSTICE

In 1884, a young black woman named Ida B. Wells boarded a Chesapeake & Ohio Railroad Company train in Memphis, Tennessee. Wells took a seat in the ladies' car. The conductor promptly ordered her to move. African Americans weren't allowed in that car. Wells would have to ride in the "black only" car, which was crowded, dirty, and filled with cigarette smoke.

Under the Civil Rights Act of 1875, it was illegal to discriminate against African Americans on trains or in any other public facility. But the law was routinely ignored in the South.

On this occasion, however, Ida Wells refused to go along with the injustice. She wouldn't budge. The conductor "tried to drag me out of the seat," she would recall, "but the moment he caught hold of my arm I fastened my teeth in the back of his hand."

Ida B. Wells-Barnett (1862–1931) was a journalist and activist for civil rights and women's rights. She is best known for her anti-lynching campaign, but also was critical of Booker T. Washington's policy of accommodation, and helped to found the NAACP.

Ida B. Wells was born in Mississippi in 1862. When she was 14, her parents and one of her sisters died in a yellow fever epidemic. After that, she supported her five surviving siblings. Eventually, they moved to Memphis to live with an aunt. Wells attended college and became a teacher.

It was while traveling from Memphis to her teaching job in Shelby County that Wells had her confrontation with the train conductor. After having his hand bitten, the conductor was intimidated enough not to try to remove Wells by himself. He enlisted help from a baggage handler and another man. Together the three men pulled Wells out of the car. The white passengers cheered.

Wells sued the Chesapeake & Ohio Railroad. She won a $500 judgment in the local courts. But the decision was overturned by a Tennessee state court. That setback didn't discourage Wells from fighting for equal rights. Newspapers asked her to write about her experiences. She started a new career as a journalist and an activist for civil rights.

Wells became part owner of a newspaper, *Free Speech and Headlight*, in 1889. She used the paper to promote the cause of justice and equality. In its pages, she called for women to be given the right to vote. She also condemned racism and violence against African Americans. As a result of her courageous stand against lynching, Wells would be forced to leave Memphis.

A CRUSADE AGAINST LYNCHING

Wells had three African-American friends who opened a small grocery store in Memphis. White-owned stores didn't appreciate the competition for business. They repeatedly threatened Wells's friends. But the black men refused to close down. Finally, a white mob attacked the grocery store. In trying to defend their property, Wells's friends shot a member of the mob and were promptly arrested.

The following night, a large white mob descended on the jail. The mob dragged the three black storeowners from their cells and brutally lynched them.

Ida Wells was stunned. But she felt that as a journalist, she had a duty to write about the murders. She produced a scathing editorial in *Free Speech and Headlight*. In it she noted that the city of Memphis refused to do anything to protect black people from white violence. It wouldn't even permit blacks to defend themselves. "There is therefore," Wells wrote, "only one thing left that we can to do; save our money and leave a town which will neither protect our lives and property, nor give us a fair trial in the courts, but takes us out and murders us in cold blood when accused by white persons."

The editorial galvanized the African-American community in Memphis. But Wells wasn't done. She launched an in-depth investigation of lynching throughout the United States. Wells concluded that the real cause of lynching wasn't anger over crimes committed by black men against white victims. Rather, she said, lynching was "an excuse to get rid of [blacks] who were acquiring wealth and property and thus keep the race terrorized."

Fury at what Wells wrote led whites to attack and destroy the

═ Did You Know? ═

In 1930, shortly before her death, Ida B. Wells ran for the Illinois state senate. She lost the election. But as one of the first African-American women ever to run for public office, she helped pave the way for future black women candidates.

offices of her newspaper. For her own safety, she had to move from Memphis. She settled in Chicago. There, Wells continued writing and speaking about lynching, segregation, and women's rights. In 1896, she became one of the founding members of the National Association of Colored Women. The organization worked for the causes of women's and children's rights. Ida Wells ran to become its president in 1924, but she didn't win. The woman who won was Mary McLeod Bethune.

EDUCATOR AND PRESIDENTIAL ADVISER

Mary McLeod was born in South Carolina in 1875. Her parents were former slaves. As a young girl, she worked on a farm and went to a school run by a Christian missionary. When she got home from school, she would teach her school lessons to her family.

Mary McLeod Bethune (1875–1955) was a nationally known advocate for the education of African Americans. She also served as an adviser to President Franklin D. Roosevelt.

Mary McLeod wanted to become a missionary and travel to Africa. But black women didn't become missionaries in those days. She graduated from college and became a teacher. She taught at several schools for a few years. She also married Albertus Bethune. Then, in 1904, she decided to open her own school.

In the early 1900s, Daytona Beach, Florida, was the site of a new railroad project. Many African Americans had moved to the area, hoping to find work. Mary McLeod Bethune was determined to give the daughters of these people the opportunity for a decent education. At the time, it wasn't uncommon for black children to receive no formal schooling.

Bethune opened the Daytona Literary and Industrial School for Training Negro Girls in 1904. It had six students—five girls and Bethune's son. They used crates for desks and charcoal for pencils. To raise money, they baked pies and sold them to construction workers.

But the school grew, and Bethune was able to raise more money for it. More and more girls enrolled. In 1923, it merged with a boys' school. In 1929, this coeducational school became Bethune-Cookman College. Mary McLeod Bethune was its president for many years.

Education was Bethune's passion, but she also fought for civil rights for blacks and for women. She often rode her bicycle around Daytona Beach, asking for money to help blacks pay poll taxes so that they could vote. And as Bethune-Cookman grew, she become famous and was able to launch new projects. She founded the National Council of Negro Women in 1935. Its goal was to improve the lives of black women. The organization continues to work toward that goal today.

In 1936, President Franklin D. Roosevelt made Bethune the director of African American affairs in the National Youth Administration. One of her jobs was to help create more employment opportunities for young blacks. She also gave the president advice on working with the African-American community. She was a member of Roosevelt's "Black Cabinet," a group of African-American advisers to the president.

"On Our Way"

Mary McLeod Bethune died in 1955 in Daytona Beach, Florida. The year before, the United States Supreme Court ruled that blacks and whites could not be segregated in schools. When Bethune had started her career as an educator, such a decision would have been unthinkable.

"We are on our way," Bethune wrote in a newspaper column. "But these are frontiers which we must conquer. . . . We must gain full equality in education . . . in economic opportunity, and full equality in the abundance of life."

On December 1, 1955, Rosa Parks was arrested and charged with disorderly conduct in Montgomery, Alabama, for refusing to give up her bus seat to a white passenger. Her arrest and $14 fine for violating a city ordinance led African-American bus riders and others to boycott the Montgomery city buses. The boycott lasted for one year and brought the Civil Rights Movement worldwide attention.

4

STRIKE AND BOYCOTT

In 1896, the U.S. Supreme Court handed down a decision in a case known as *Plessy v. Ferguson*. At issue in the case was a Louisiana law that prohibited black passengers from riding in the same railway cars as white passengers. Was this a violation of the 14th Amendment to the Constitution, which required states to give all their citizens equal protection under the law? No, the Supreme Court said in its Plessy decision. Segregation on trains was legal. The "black" railway cars simply had to be on a par with the "white" cars.

The significance of the *Plessy* decision extended well beyond trains. The ruling established a legal basis for segregation: "separate but equal" treatment of the races. Southern states soon passed a host of "Jim Crow" laws. These laws kept blacks apart from whites in public facilities, including buses, hotels, restaurants, theaters, restrooms, pools, and even schools.

Of course, "separate but equal" was a fiction. The public facilities provided for whites were almost always better than those provided for blacks. This unjust situation would exist for nearly 60 years before it was successfully challenged in the courts.

STRIKE FOR EQUALITY

In 1951, the students at Robert Russa Moton High School gathered for an assembly. Most of them didn't know what the assembly was about. Then Barbara Johns took the stage. She was 16 and a junior at the school. Barbara had told only a few trusted friends about her plan. They agreed not to tell their teachers or their parents. "We knew we had to do it ourselves," Barbara said, "and that if we had asked for adult help before taking the first step, we would have been turned down."

First Barbara asked all the teachers to leave the assembly. Then she told her fellow students the plan: she wanted them all to go on strike.

Moton High was in Farmville, Virginia. Only African-American kids went there. White kids had their own high school. The white school had up-to-date science labs and new books. It had a big athletic field and plenty of supplies.

Moton High was built to hold about 180 students. Enrollment topped 400 in 1951. Some classes were taught in school buses. Parents complained. So the school board put up a few tar-paper shacks to hold the overflow. Moton High didn't have a cafeteria or a gym. It didn't have lockers. Books were old and torn.

Barbara Johns said this was wrong. Segregated schools were supposed to be equal. Johns told her fellow students they should demand their rights. They should demand a new Moton High that was just as good as the white high school. Until the school board promised to build such a school, Johns said, Moton's students should walk out. The assembled students agreed. The strike was on.

(Right) Portrait of 16-year-old Barbara Johns, who in 1951 organized the boycott at Robert Russa Moton High School in Virginia, which is pictured above.

SEPARATE ISN'T EQUAL

The students stayed out on strike for two weeks. Almost all their parents supported them. In the meantime, Barbara Johns and others contacted lawyers from the NAACP. At first the civil rights organization didn't seem interested. But Johns wouldn't take no for an answer, and the NAACP finally agreed to take the case. But there was a condition: the students had to sue for an integrated school, not a separate but equal one. The students agreed.

The NAACP had been challenging public school segregation for a long time. It had occasionally won cases in state courts. Always, though, these victories were overturned on appeal.

The Sit-In Movement

The strategy of nonviolence would help to desegregate American lunch counters. In most places in the South, blacks could not sit at the lunch counters of local department stores or neighborhood restaurants. In 1960, four young black men—Franklin McCain, Joseph McNeil, Ezell Blair, Jr., and David Richmond—decided to challenge this discrimination. They were freshmen at the blacks-only Agricultural and Technical State University in Greensboro, North Carolina. On February 1 the four entered the downtown F. W. Woolworth department store. The business catered to both blacks and whites. But the lunch counter was open only to whites. After making purchases in the store, the four young men sat down at the lunch counter and tried to order food.

The white waitress told the men that she could not serve blacks. The manager asked them to leave. But the four stayed seated. They quietly waited at the counter until the store closed. And they returned the next day. This time they were accompanied by about 20 more students, including four women. Local newspapers and TV news programs reported the story. They kept returning, and more people joined the protest each day.

As news of the Greensboro protests spread, students organized sit-ins in other North Carolina cities and in other states. In some cases, African American students were joined by white students. When students were arrested, others took their place. The sit-in movement eventually led to the passage of legislation that ended segregation policies in restaurants, theaters, and concert halls in many southern states.

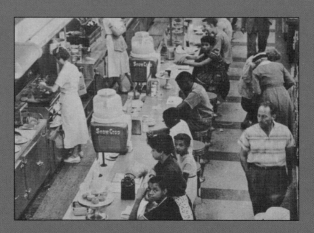

The issue of school segregation finally landed before the U.S. Supreme Court in 1952 and 1953. Five different cases were combined. One of those cases involved Moton High, where Barbara Johns had organized a strike by students. The combined case was called *Brown v. the Board of Education of Topeka*.

The NAACP's lead attorney was the brilliant Thurgood Marshall. He argued that school segregation violated the equal protection clause of the 14th Amendment. Segregated schools weren't equal, and they could never be made equal, Marshall said.

In May 1954, the Supreme Court handed down its decision in *Brown v. Board of Education*. "Segregation of white and colored children in public schools," the decision read, "has a detrimental effect upon the colored children. . . . We conclude that, in the field of public education, the doctrine of 'separate but equal' has no place." All nine justices were in agreement.

Attorneys George E. C. Hayes (left), Thurgood Marshall (center), and James M. Nabrit (right) celebrate outside the U.S. Supreme Court building after the Court ruled in May 1954 that school segregation was unconstitutional. In 1967, Marshall (1908–1993) would become the first African American to serve as a Supreme Court justice.

A CONSTITUTIONAL RIGHT

After the Supreme Court ruling, some public schools became integrated peacefully. But many others, especially in the South, did not. Southern cities and towns formed white citizens' councils. They used violence and intimidation to prevent black students from trying to enroll in white schools.

And the Supreme Court's *Brown v. Board of Education* decision applied only to segregation in public schools. Other Jim Crow laws remained unchanged.

In 1955, Claudette Colvin was a 15-year-old living in Montgomery, Alabama. She had to ride a city bus to and from school. She knew that if you were black, you were supposed to give up your seat to a white passenger. It didn't matter if you were there first. It didn't matter if there were no "black" seats left at the back of the bus. In that case, you had to stand.

Colvin had been studying black history in school. She had been learning about the U.S. Constitution. One day, when the bus driver told her to give up her seat to a white passenger, she refused. "It's my constitutional right to sit here," she declared.

The bus driver called the police. Colvin was arrested. She spent the night in jail.

BOYCOTT

Nine months after Claudette Colvin refused to give up her seat, another African-American woman, Rosa Parks, did the same thing. She also was arrested. This time, leaders of Montgomery's African-American community took action. To protest Parks's treatment, they called on all blacks to stay off city buses for one day. An estimated 90 percent of Montgomery's African-American bus riders participated in the one-day boycott.

After that first day, thousands of black citizens went to a meeting called by the Montgomery Improvement Association (MIA). The MIA, made up of black community and church leaders, was headed by a young pastor named Martin Luther King Jr. At the meeting, the black citizens agreed to

an ongoing boycott of Montgomery's buses. They wouldn't ride the buses again until the buses were integrated.

The boycott stretched into weeks and then months. Most of Montgomery's African Americans participated. Some walked to work or to school. Others rode in taxis owned by blacks. Black churches also bought cars and set up car pools.

While the boycott was taking place, civil rights lawyers took the case to court. They argued that segregated buses were just as unconstitutional as segregated schools. Four black women testified in that case. One of them was Claudette Colvin.

The case went to the Supreme Court. In November 1956, the Court agreed that bus segregation wasn't permissible under the Constitution. The Montgomery bus boycott ended when the Supreme Court decision took effect a month later. The boycott had lasted 381 days.

Rosa Parks

Rosa Parks was 42 years old in December 1955, when she refused to give up her bus seat. Parks was a seamstress. Her husband was a barber. They both did work for the Montgomery chapter of the NAACP.

For years, the story circulated that Rosa Parks had refused to move from her seat because she was exhausted and her feet ached after a long day of work. In a 1994 book, however, Parks said that the story was incorrect. "Our mistreatment was just not right, and I was tired of it," she wrote. Her courage gave hope and determination to other activists.

On August 28, 1963, approximately 250,000 people took part in the March on Washington, DC, for Jobs and Freedom. At the political rally African American leaders called for greater civil and economic rights for blacks, as well as racial harmony.

5

PATHS TO FREEDOM

The Montgomery bus boycott ended on December 20, 1956. One of the first African Americans to ride a bus that day was Martin Luther King Jr. Other civil rights activists had chosen King to be their spokesman during the boycott. His speeches and sermons rallied the black community. He gave them courage to stick with the boycott.

In the years after the boycott, King became one of the most important leaders of the civil rights movement. Millions of people admired him. But many racists hated him and wanted to stop his work. King received many threats. Once, his home was bombed. But he always urged people not to fight violence with violence. He believed in the power of peaceful protest. His courage and strength convinced hundreds of thousands of others to believe in it, too.

A NEW DECADE

It was the 1960s. Jim Crow laws had been removed. African Americans were supposed to be able to sit anywhere on a bus or a train. They could not be forced to use separate restrooms or water fountains. Also, African Americans didn't have to pass a literacy test in order to vote. They supposedly had equal rights. That was the law.

Unfortunately, states in the Deep South ignored the law. So African Americans took action again. Many white people joined them. Like Martin Luther King Jr., they were peaceful. They were just following the law.

RIDING FOR FREEDOM

In May of 1961, seven African Americans and six white Americans boarded two public buses in Washington, D.C. The buses were bound for states deep in the South. The 13 passengers were testing their constitutional right to integrated buses and bus stops. They called themselves the Freedom Riders.

The man who organized the Freedom Ride was James L. Farmer. He grew up in Mississippi and Texas. He said he first realized he was "colored" when his mother explained why he couldn't have a soft drink at the drug store's lunch counter. Blacks were not allowed. In college, he had to sit in the balcony at the movies. He called it the "buzzard's roost."

After college, Jim Farmer began to work for a civil rights group called CORE, the Congress for Racial Equality. He became its national director. Soon after that, he organized the first Freedom Ride.

James L. Farmer

A HARD ROAD

The Freedom Riders planned to go from the nation's capital all the way to New Orleans. The trip went well for a while. The riders were served at stations in Virginia, North Carolina, and South Carolina. Then they rolled into Alabama. There, trouble hit. Groups of angry whites were waiting. They hurled rocks at both buses. They slashed the tires of one. When the bus stopped to change tires, it was firebombed. Riders were beaten with pipes and baseball bats as they escaped the burning bus.

The riders were attacked and beaten again in Birmingham, Alabama. The Ku Klux Klan threatened to bomb them. Many of the riders were flown to safety. But new volunteers quickly replaced them. One of those volun-

teers was a young African American named John Lewis.

John Lewis admired Martin Luther King Jr. for his leadership during the Montgomery bus boycott. He shared King's belief in nonviolence. He believed strongly in civil rights. In college, he helped organize peaceful sit-ins at segregated lunch counters. He and other black students had a right to sit down and be served. Instead, they were spat on and insulted. Some were beaten and arrested.

John Lewis

But John Lewis wasn't going to give up. He climbed aboard a bus and became a Freedom Rider. The buses proceeded to Montgomery. "The bus drove into the parking deck at the station," recalled Lewis, "opened the door, and the moment, the very moment that we started down the steps of the bus, this mob came out of nowhere."

There were more than a thousand people in the mob. "You could see baseball bats; you could see hammers; you could see pieces of chain," another rider said. "You knew why they were there."

John Lewis was badly beaten. Another rider was nearly killed.

Members of the "Washington Freedom Riders Committee," enroute to Washington, D.C., hang signs from bus side windows to protest segregation as they travel through New York City, 1961.

> **= Did You Know? =**
>
> In 1986, John Lewis ran for and was elected to the U.S. House of Representatives from his district in Georgia. He has been reelected ever since.

Blacks and whites around the country and the world were shocked by the violence. They admired the Freedom Riders' courage. The riders were willing to be beaten and jailed for doing what they had the right to do.

The Freedom Rides kept going through the summer. By the time they ended, more than 500 people had ridden into the South for the cause of freedom.

THE MARCH ON WASHINGTON

On August 28, 1963, John Lewis stood in front of the Lincoln Memorial in Washington, D.C. It was the day of the March on Washington for Jobs and Freedom. Hundreds of thousands of people—black and white—had come to the U.S. capital. They were there to support civil and economic rights for African Americans.

Martin Luther King Jr. was the main speaker. He lifted everyone's hopes when he talked about his dreams of a peaceful, integrated country.

John Lewis was only 23 when he spoke that day. Unlike King, he was not famous. But he had the same dreams. He had been beaten and jailed for trying to make them come true. In his speech, Lewis said that the nation "must seek more than civil rights; we must work for the community of love, peace and true brotherhood. Our minds, souls and hearts cannot rest until freedom and justice exist for all people."

FREEDOM SUMMER

If you lived in Mississippi in 1964 and you were black, it was not easy to vote. First you had to register at the courthouse. You had to fill out a long form with 20 questions. You had to copy any section of the state's constitution. Then you had to explain what it meant—in writing.

Many blacks in Mississippi were poor and uneducated. Most of them

(Top) NAACP executive secretary Roy Wilkins (second row, center) walks with other activists during the August 1963 "March on Washington for Jobs and Freedom." Wilkins (1901–1981) was an NAACP leader for more than 40 years.

(Right) Bayard Rustin, pictured at left, speaks with fellow March on Washington organizer Cleveland Robinson. Rustin (1912–1987) had studied nonviolence as a means to achieve social change, and he helped to introduce this approach to Martin Luther King and other leaders of the Civil Rights Movement of the 1950s and 1960s.

Council Of Federated Organizations

9698 MAR-4'64

1017 Lynch Street

P.O. Box 2896

(601) 352-9605

Jackson, Mississippi 39203

March 1, 1964

Mr. Roy Wilkins, Executive Secretary
National Association for the Advancement of
                    Colored People
20 West 40 Street
New York, New York 10018

Aaron Henry
President

Robert Moses
Program Director

David Dennis
Assistant Program Director

Congressional District Coordinators

*Frank Smith, 1st
Columbus*

*James Jones, 2nd
Greenwood*

*Jesse Harris, 3rd
Vicksburg*

*Matteo Suarez 4th
Meridian*

*Lawrence Guyot, 5th
Hattiesburg*

State Office Coordinator
Charles Cobb, Jackson

Welfare and Relief Committee
*Vera Pigee, Clarksdale
Annelle Ponder, Greenwood*

Political Program Committee
Lawrence G Guyot, Hattiesburg

Finance Committee
Rev. R. L. T. Smith, Jackson

Federal Programs Committee
Jesse Morris, Jackson

Dear Mr. Wilkins:

Enclosed is a report of the Mississippi Freedom
Summer program drawn up by the staff of the Council
of Federated Organizations (COFO), which is a federa-
tion of all the national civil rights organizations
active in Mississippi. Since the NAACP is an integral
part of COFO, I'm sure you are familiar with its program.

COFO is holding a conference on March 15, 1964, to
which it invites all national civil rights leaders, to
coordinate their efforts in one direction for the
proposed Mississippi Freedom Summer program.

It is extremely vital that you try to schedule the
afternoon of March 15, 1964, to attend the COFO
conference in Jackson, Mississippi, beginning at
11:00 a.m., along with other national leaders. James
Farmer, James Forman, Whitney Young and Rev. Martin
Luther King are also being invited in order to estab-
lish and project each other's views for working together
on a joint COFO project, and make all plans and decisions
in common.

Since a press conference is being called after the
conference, we feel it is imperative that all national
civil rights organizations be present in order that
the statements issued will be representative of our
program. We feel that your joint efforts together in
Jackson would lend valuable impetus throughout the
nation for the Mississippi Freedom Summer project.

The agenda for the COFO conference for each national

The first page of a letter from Robert Moses, Council of Federated Organizations's program
director, to NAACP Executive Secretary Roy Wilkins regarding the 1964 Mississippi Freedom
Summer project.

Medgar W. Evers (1925–1963) led voter registration drives and fought segregation in Mississippi during the 1950s and early 1960s. In June 1963 he was murdered by a white man.

couldn't qualify to vote. A group called the Student Nonviolent Coordinating Committee (SNCC) decided to try to change that. SNCC (pronounced "SNICK") was started by college students in Tennessee. The students had first organized sit-ins at lunch counters in many southern towns. SNCC now decided to tackle the issue of voting rights. SNCC organizers called their project Freedom Summer.

Freedom Summer had many goals. The top goal was to help more blacks in Mississippi register to vote. Other goals were to open community centers, help black kids with reading and math, and start a new political party that would listen to the needs of African Americans.

College students from around the country volunteered to take part in the project. Many, but not all, were white. After a training session, the first group headed for Mississippi. Not long after that, three volunteers disappeared. Their bodies were found buried together almost two months later. They had been murdered.

The murders frightened other volunteers. But it didn't stop them. Freedom Summer kept on. It didn't achieve all its goals. But it would make a big difference in the lives of blacks in Mississippi. Less than 7 percent of black voters were registered in 1964. By 1969, that number had jumped to more than 66 percent.

= Did You Know? =

In 2005, a Mississippi jury convicted a former Ku Klux Klan member of the murders of the three Freedom Summer volunteers.

ANOTHER WAY

Not all African-American activists believed in nonviolence. One of those who didn't was Malcolm X.

Malcolm X was born Malcolm Little in 1925. He changed his last name when he joined an African-American religious group called the Nation of Islam. Malcolm X was a powerful speaker. His words and ideas excited many young African Americans. He made them proud to be black.

Landmark Laws

In 1964, President Lyndon Johnson signed the Civil Rights Act. It outlawed discrimination in all public places based on race, color, religion, or national origin. The act also made it illegal to discriminate in hiring people for jobs. It gave strength to the laws by creating the Equal Opportunity Commission to make sure that they were followed.

President Johnson signed another major law a year later. The Voting Rights Act of 1965 finally outlawed all the ways that state and local governments had kept African Americans from voting. Rosa Parks stood with the president as he signed the bill into law.

President Lyndon B. Johnson signs the Voting Rights Act as Martin Luther King Jr. (center), Rosa Parks (right, in hat) and other civil rights activists look on, August 6, 1965.

Two of the most important activists of the 1960s were Dr. Martin Luther King Jr. (left, 1929–1968) and Malcolm X (1925–1965).

Malcolm X thought nonviolence was fine—if it worked. But if it didn't, then he thought black people should fight back against oppression. In one of his speeches, he said, "Be peaceful, be courteous, obey the law, respect everyone; but if someone puts his hand on you, send him to the cemetery."

Malcolm X didn't believe that white people would ever grant blacks equality. The solution, he thought, was for blacks to create their own society, separate from that of whites.

In 1964, Malcolm X left the Nation of Islam. He became a follower of traditional Islam. He went on a pilgrimage to Mecca, Saudi Arabia. Mecca is Islam's holy city. On the pilgrimage, Malcolm X saw people of all races and backgrounds treating one another with dignity and respect. He began to change his mind about race relations. He came to believe that blacks and whites in America—and around the world—could live peacefully together.

He didn't have a chance to work very long for his new beliefs. He was assassinated in 1965 as he was starting to give a speech in New York City.

The Reverend Jesse Jackson (b. 1941) is one of the most important and influential African American activists working today.

6

INTO THE FUTURE

The struggle for African American civil rights was long and painful. But by the late 1960s, Jim Crow was gone. The Civil Rights and Voting Rights Acts made discrimination illegal. Blacks in the South could vote without fear, and many more were registering. African Americans were running in local, state, and national races—and getting elected. Activists had worked hard for these causes. Many had been hurt. Some had been killed.

Activists had succeeded. But the struggle wasn't over. Racism still existed. So did discrimination, even if it was not as obvious as before. There was still work to be done.

JESSE JACKSON

Jesse Jackson was born in South Carolina in 1941. His activism began in 1960 when he tried to desegregate the local public library. He started working for Martin Luther King Jr.'s civil rights organization in 1965. He directed Operation Breadbasket. Its goal was social and economic justice. Jackson was in Memphis, Tennessee, when King was assassinated there on April 4, 1968. The killing shocked everyone. But neither Jackson nor the other civil rights activists who had worked with King were going to give up.

In 1971, Jackson created Operation PUSH (People United to Serve Humanity). This group worked to improve the conditions of black communities. Later, he founded the National Rainbow Coalition. Its goal was equal rights for all Americans. The two groups came together later as the Rainbow PUSH Coalition.

Jackson believed that civil rights mattered everywhere, not just in the United States. He traveled to South Africa in 1979 to speak out against that country's racist, white-controlled government. He also went to troubled nations where Americans had been taken hostage. His work helped get American hostages freed in Syria, Iraq, and Yugoslavia.

In 1984, Jackson decided to run for the Democratic Party's nomination for president of the United States. He finished third. Four year later, Jackson ran again. This time, he won the primary voting in nine states, plus the District of Columbia. In the six-person race, Jackson finished second, behind only Michael Dukakis. For the first time in U.S. history, an African American had mounted a presidential campaign with a serious chance at winning.

NEW ACTIVISM

Jesse Jackson has tried to make a difference in many areas. Many younger black activists have started to do the same thing. They believe the fight for civil rights needs to be about more than one group of people. Majora Carter has fought to make sure we all have a clean environment.

Majora Carter was born in New York City in 1966. She grew up at a time when many cities were in terrible shape. Her neighborhood in the South Bronx was one of the worst. The air was polluted. Playgrounds were crumbling and filthy. Garbage seemed to be dumped everywhere. Carter decided to do something about it.

GREEN NEIGHBORHOODS

After college, Carter returned to her childhood neighborhood and got to work. She insisted that everyone deserves the right to live in a clean and

Jesse Jackson (left) marches with fellow activists Roslyn Brock and the Reverend Al Sharpton during a demonstration in March 2012. Sharpton (b. 1954) has been controversial but effective in his efforts to draw public attention to injustices against African Americans. Brock (b. 1965) became chairperson of the NAACP in February 2010, becoming the youngest person to serve in that position.

safe environment. Carter convinced the government of New York City to abandon a plan to dump waste in her South Bronx neighborhood. Then she helped get money from the government to build bike paths. The paths would connect different parts of the South Bronx. The money also created a program to help local businesses. After all that, Carter became involved in building the first new waterfront park the South Bronx had seen in many years.

Van Jones, former Obama administration adviser for Green Jobs, Enterprise and Innovation, speaks at the Mobilization to End Poverty conference April 27, 2009 in Washington, DC.

In 2001, Carter started Sustainable South Bronx. The group helped train people for new careers in the environmental field. And in 2008, she created the Majora Carter Group (MCG). MCG helps connect governments and businesses so they can work together to solve environmental problems in cities and neighborhoods.

"There are South Bronxes all over the country," Carter says. "I believe you shouldn't have to leave your neighborhood to live in a better one."

GREEN JOBS

For Van Jones, today's struggle is for human rights against poverty and pollution. Jones believes that green jobs can help the poor out of poverty and save the environment at the same time.

Van Jones was born in Tennessee in 1968. He has worked for years to help retrain people in the green-jobs field. Jobs in solar and wind energy and urban gardening all help the environment and give people work.

In 2009, President Barack Obama appointed Jones as a special adviser on green jobs. In that post, Jones searched for new ways to help Americans save money on energy costs. He worked to stop pollution from power plants. And he started a program to help people make their homes "greener" and safer from weather disasters. A lot of his work focused on rural Americans and racial minorities. When he left the Obama administration, Jones joined the Center for American Progress and became the head of its green-jobs program.

FROM CIVIL RIGHTS TO EATING RIGHT

Like Majora Carter and Van Jones, Bryant Terry is an activist for civil rights and human rights. But Terry does something different. He cooks.

Bryant Terry is an eco-chef. He uses popular culture and modern media to encourage people to eat healthier and find joy in food and cooking. He works to make people more aware of food and its connection to natural resources.

In 2008–09, Terry started the Southern Organic Kitchen Project. The project helped teach people about the dangers of unhealthy eating. It also helped them learn about healthier, alternative food. One of Terry's goals is to make healthy food more affordable to everyone, especially the poor. He has written two books. He also has a website and blogs regularly about his work.

> = *Did You Know?* =
>
> In 2008, Van Jones wrote *The Green Collar Economy*. His book argues that environmental jobs aren't only good for workers. They will also help make the economy stronger. The book became a bestseller.

CHAPTER NOTES

p. 9:   "We were waiting and listening . . ." Frederick Douglass, *The Life and Times of Frederick Douglass: From 1817–1882, Written by Himself; with an Introduction by the Right Hon. John Bright*. John Lobb, ed. (London: Christian Age Office, 1882), p. 308.

p. 9:   "At last . . ." Ibid.

p. 10:   "all persons held as slaves . . ." Emancipation Proclamation, January 1, 1863. http://www.archives.gov/exhibits/featured_documents/emancipation_proclamation/transcript.html

p. 10:   "the entire abolition . . ." Douglass, *Life and Times of Frederick Douglass*, p. 309.

p. 12:   "I dropped into the ranks . . ." Ibid., p. 184.

p. 15:   "Slavery is not abolished until . . ." Frederick Douglass, *Frederick Douglass: Selected Speeches and Writings*, edited by Philip S. Foner (Chicago: Chicago Review Press, 1999), p. 578.

p. 17:   "I seem to be living . . ." Sharman Apt Russell and Heather Lehr Wagner, *Frederick Douglass: Abolitionist Editor* (Infobase Publishing, 2005), p. 71.

p. 20:   "My mother, who was . . ." Booker T. Washington, *Up from Slavery: An Autobiography* (New York: Doubleday, Page & Co. 1907), p. 21.

p. 22:   "progress in the enjoyment . . ." "Booker T. Washington Delivers the 1895 Atlanta Compromise Speech," History Matters: The U.S. Survey Course on the Web. http://historymatters.gmu.edu/d/39/

p. 25:   "We are men! . . ." William Evitts, "The Niagara Movement," Buffalo and Erie County Historical Society, 2004. http://www.buffaloah.com/h/niag.html

p. 25:   "I am resolved . . ." William Edward Burghardt Du Bois, *The Wisdom of W. E. B. Du Bois*, edited by Aberjhani (New York: Kensington Publishing Corp., 2003), pp. xiv–xv.

p. 27:   "tried to drag me . . ." Jackson Lears, *Rebirth of a Nation: The Making of Modern America, 1877–1920* (New York: HarperCollins, 2009), p. 130.

p. 29:   "There is therefore only . . ." Paula J. Giddings, *Ida: A Sword Among Lions* (New York: HarperCollins, 2008), p. 189.

p. 29:   "an excuse to get rid . . ." Philip Dray, *At the Hands of Persons Unknown: The Lynching of Black America* (New York: Random House, 2003), p. 63.

p. 31:   "We are on our way. . ." Anja Schüler, "Mary McLeod Bethune," in *Encyclopedia of African American History*, Vol. 1 (New York: Oxford University Press, 2009), p. 176.

p. 34:   "We knew we had . . ." The Martin Luther King, Jr. Research and Education Institute at Stanford University, "The Children's Crusade" (curriculum guide). http://www.stanford.edu/group/King/liberation_curriculum/children-scrusade/additionalactivities.htm#part1

p. 37:   "Segregation of white . . ." PBS, *The Rise and Fall of Jim Crow*, "Brown v. Board of Education (1954)." http://www.pbs.org/wnet/jim-crow/stories_events_brown.html

p. 38:   "It's my constitutional right . . ." Margot Adler, "Before Rosa Parks, There Was Claudette Colvin," NPR Weekend Edition Sunday, March 15, 2009. http://www.npr.org/templates/story/story.php?storyId=101719889

p. 39:   "Our mistreatment . . ." Rosa Parks, *Quiet Strength* (Zondervan Publishing House, 1994), p. 22.

p. 43:   "The bus drove into . . ." Ann Bausum, "Freedom Riders: John Lewis and Jim Zwerg on the Front Lines of the Civil Rights Movement." http://www.annbausum.com/freedom_rides.html

p. 43:   "You could see baseball bats . . ." Ibid.

p. 44:   "must seek more than . . ." John Lewis, with Michael D'Orso. *Walking with the Wind: A Memoir of the Movement* (New York: Simon & Schuster, 1998), p. 220.

p. 49:   "Be peaceful, be courteous . . ." Malcolm X, *Malcolm X Speaks: Selected Speeches and Statements*, edited by George Breitman (New York: Grove Press, 1965), p. 12.

p. 54:   "There are South Bronxes . . ." Majora Carter Group website. http://www.majoracartergroup.com/

CHRONOLOGY

1863   President Lincoln issues the Emancipation Proclamation on January 1.

1865   The Civil War ends. Congress passes, and the states ratify, the 13th Amendment to the Constitution. It outlaws slavery.

1866   Congress passes the 14th Amendment, which guarantees equal protection under the law for everyone, regardless of race.

1868   The 14th Amendment is ratified.

1869   Congress passes the 15th Amendment, which guarantees African-American men the right to vote.

1870   The 15th Amendment is ratified.

1881   Booker T. Washington opens the Tuskegee Institute.

1895   Washington gives his "Atlanta Compromise" speech.

1896   The Supreme Court's decision in the case of *Plessy v. Ferguson* paves the way for the system of Jim Crow laws that require racial segregation in the South. The National Association of Colored Women is founded.

1904   Mary McLeod Bethune opens the Daytona Literary and Industrial Training School for Negro Girls.

1909   The National Association for the Advancement of Colored People (NAACP) is formed.

1951   Barbara Johns leads a strike at her segregated high school in Virginia.

1954   In *Brown v. the Board of Education of Topeka*, the Supreme Court rules that racially segregated public schools are unconstitutional.

1955   African Americans launch a boycott of city buses in Montgomery, Alabama.

1956   The Supreme Court rules that public transportation must be integrated.

1964   President Johnson signs the Civil Rights Act.

1965   President Johnson signs the Voting Rights Act. Malcolm X is assassinated in New York City.

1968   Martin Luther King Jr. is assassinated in Memphis, Tennessee.

1988   Jesse Jackson finishes second in the Democratic presidential primary.

GLOSSARY

abolitionist—a person favoring the end of slavery.

amendment—a change made to a constitution or law.

boycott—to refuse to associate with, buy the products of, or use the services of a company or organization as a means of protest.

detrimental—harmful.

integrated—including people from all races.

lynch—to put someone to death outside of the law, through mob action.

oppression—the unjust or cruel use of power.

proclamation—an official and formal public announcement.

ratify—to approve formally.

secede—to withdraw from a government or organization.

segregation—the practice of keeping one group or race separated from another.

wanton—without just cause.

FURTHER READING

Bridges, Ruby, and Margo Lundell. *Through My Eyes*. New York: Scholastic, 1999.

Fradin, Dennis Brindell, and Judith Bloom. *Ida B. Wells: Mother of the Civil Rights Movement*. Boston: Houghton Mifflin, 2000.

Haskins, James. *Freedom Rides: Journey for Justice*. New York: Hyperion Books for Children, 1995.

Hoose, Phillip M. *Claudette Colvin: Twice Toward Justice*. New York: Farrar, Straus and Giroux, 2009.

Pinkney, Andrea Davis. *Let It Shine: Stories of Black Women Freedom Fighters*. Boston: Gulliver Books, 2000.

Stafford, Mark. *W. E. B. Dubois*. New York: Chelsea House, 1990.

INTERNET RESOURCES

http://www.loc.gov/exhibits/odyssey/educate/bookert.html

This page, part of the *African American Odyssey* exhibit from the Library of Congress, examines Booker T. Washington and W. E. B. Du Bois.

http://www.pbs.org/wgbh/amex/eyesontheprize/

The companion website for *Eyes on the Prize: America's Civil Rights Movement, 1954–1985*, a documentary series from PBS's American Experience.

http://www.crmvet.org/index.htm

A website dedicated to veterans of the civil rights movement.

http://www.core-online.org/History/freedom%20rides.htm

This site, from the Congress of Racial Equality, deals with the Freedom Rides.

http://americanhistory.si.edu/brown/history/4-five/farmville-virginia-1.html

The Smithsonian Institution's National Museum of American History has an online site about *Brown v. Board of Education*. This page deals with the Moton High School strike.

INDEX

Numbers in **bold italics** refer to captions.

CONTRIBUTORS

CAROL ELLIS has written several books for young people. Her subjects have included law in Ancient Greece, African American artists, the Gilded Age, endangered species and martial arts. She lives in New York.

Senior Consulting Editor **DR. MARC LAMONT HILL** is one of the leading hip-hop generation intellectuals in the country. Dr. Hill has lectured widely and provides regular commentary for media outlets like NPR, the *Washington Post*, *Essence Magazine*, the *New York Times*, CNN, MSNBC, and *The O'Reilly Factor*. He is the host of the nationally syndicated television show *Our World With Black Enterprise*. Dr. Hill is a columnist and editor-at-large for the *Philadelphia Daily News*. His books include the award-winning *Beats, Rhymes, and Classroom Life: Hip-Hop Pedagogy and the Politics of Identity* (2009).

Since 2009 Dr. Hill has been on the faculty of Columbia University as Associate Professor of Education at Teachers College. He holds an affiliated faculty appointment in African American Studies at the Institute for Research in African American Studies at Columbia University.

Since his days as a youth in Philadelphia, Dr. Hill has been a social justice activist and organizer. He is a founding board member of My5th, a non-profit organization devoted to educating youth about their legal rights and responsibilities. He is also a board member and organizer of the Philadelphia Student Union. Dr. Hill also works closely with the ACLU Drug Reform Project, focusing on drug informant policy. In addition to his political work, Dr. Hill continues to work directly with African American and Latino youth.

In 2005, *Ebony* named Dr. Hill one of America's 100 most influential Black leaders. The magazine had previously named him one of America's top 30 Black leaders under 30 years old.